SAGITTARIUS

November 22 ... ?1

The secret *of* getting ahead *is* getting started.

✧ Mark Twain ✧

CARNATION

autumn

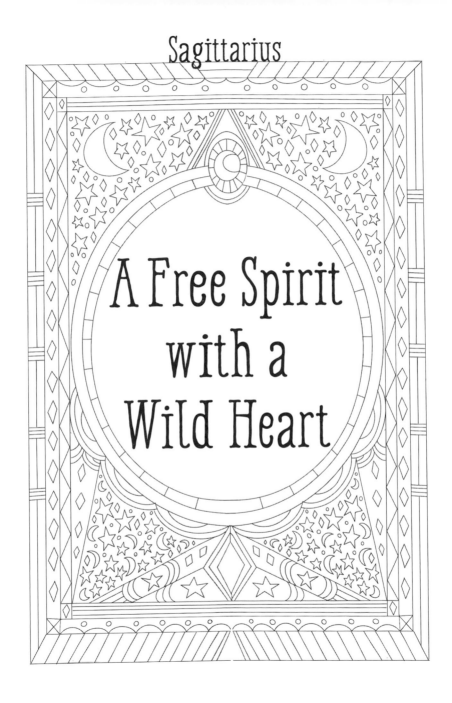

Sagittarius

A Free Spirit
with a
Wild Heart

☆Sagittarius☆

♃

Ruled by Jupiter

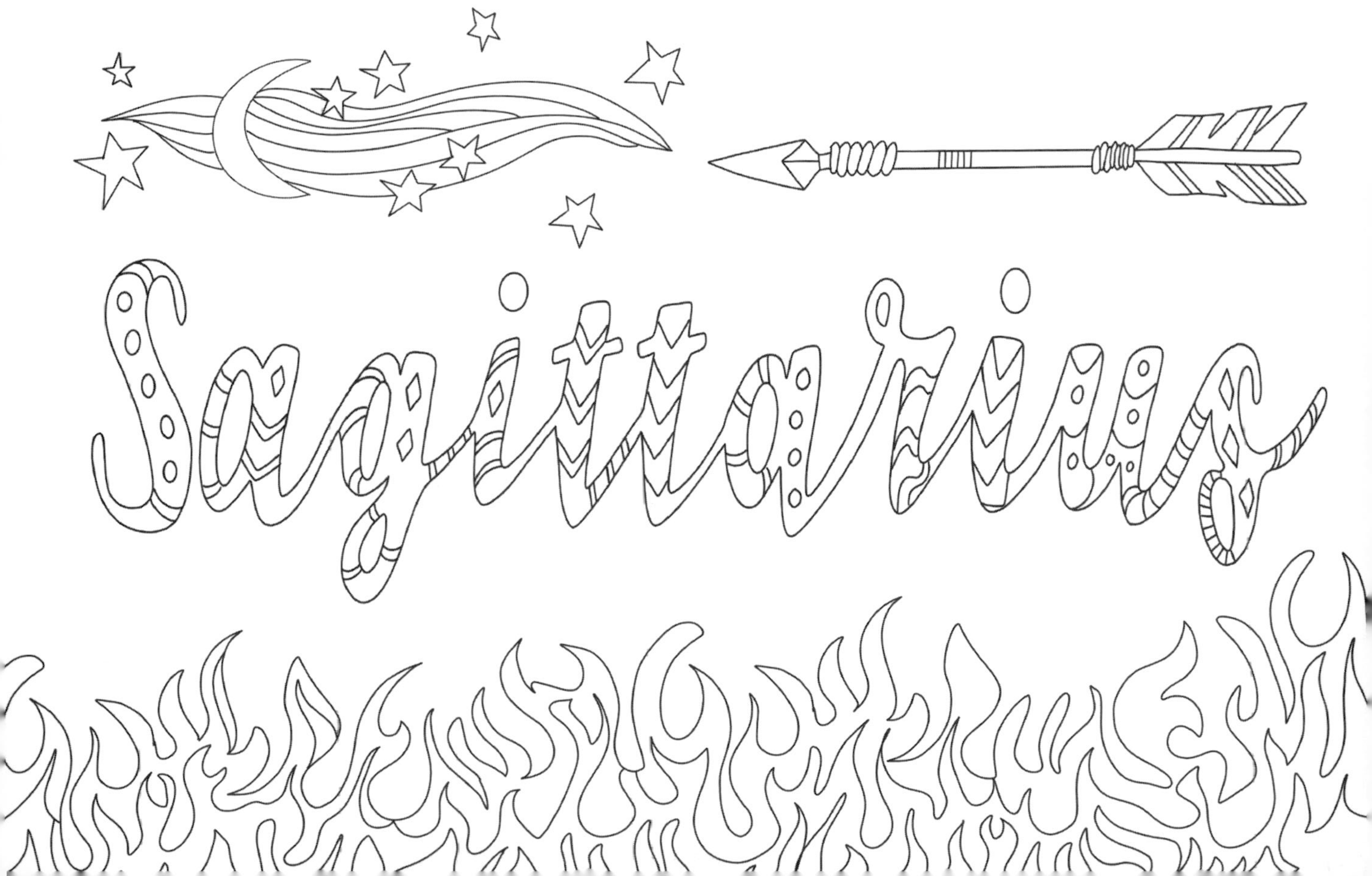
Sagittarius

RULING HOUSE

9

The House of Philosophy

SAGITTARIUS

✧

Whatever I set my sights on I go after

✧✧✧

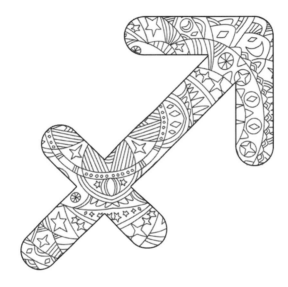

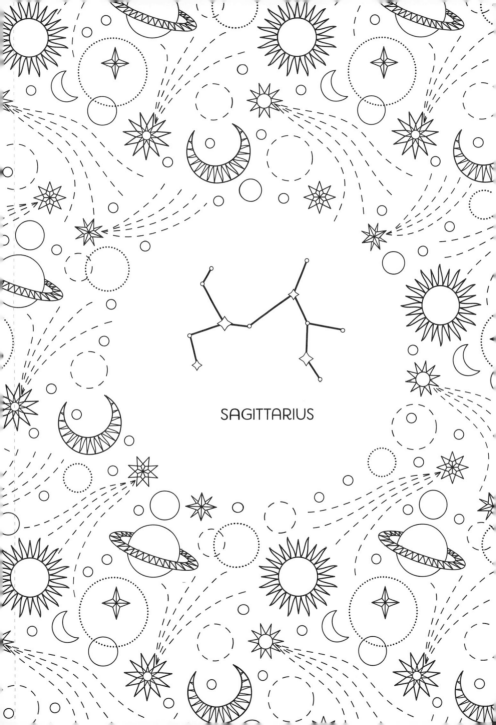

SAGITTARIUS

Aries

Taurus

Gemini

Cancer

Leo

Virgo

Libra

Scorpio

Sagittarius

Capricorn

Aquarius

Pisces

Fire Signs

Aries

Leo

Sagittarius

LET THE STARS LEAD THE WAY